SOFT CANOPIES

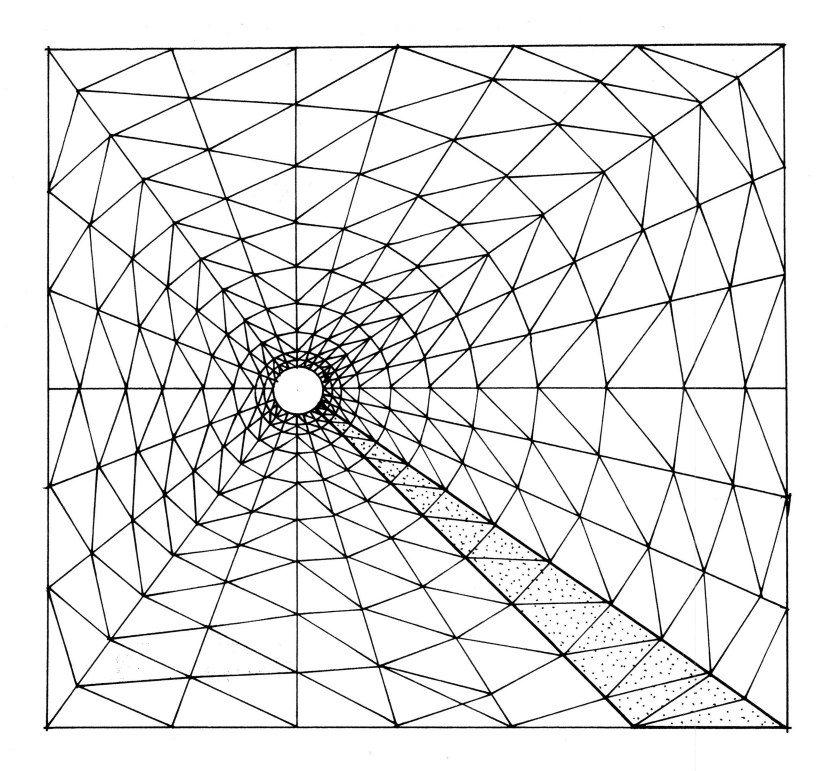

SOFT CANOPIES

MARITZ VANDENBERG

DETAIL IN BUILDING

A.D. ACADEMY EDITIONS

DETAIL IN BUILDING

Advisory Panel: Maritz Vandenberg, Christopher Dean, Christopher McCarthy, Michael Spens

ACKNOWLEDGEMENTS

The following people, listed alphabetically, have given me invaluable assistance. For this I thank them, though all mistakes are of course my own.

Helen Elias of Buro Happold; Brian Forster of Ove Arup and Partners; Joe Gardias of McCalls Special Products; Tony Hunt of Anthony Hunt Associates; Ben Kaser of Sonderkonstruktionen und Leichtbau; Alistair Lenczner of Ove Arup and Partners; Tim MacFarlane of Dewhurst MacFarlane and Partners; Patrick Morreau of Ove Arup and Partners; Eddie Pugh of Buro Happold; Lance Rowell of Landrell Fabric Engineering Limited; William Taylor of Sir Michael Hopkins and Partners; Neil Thomas of Atelier One; John Thornton of Ove Arup and Partners; John Walton of Bridon International Limited.

All illustrations are credited on page 63. I am particularly grateful to Timothy and Lorna Soar for allowing me to use their photographs of Buckingham Palace ticket office.

Finally I wish to record my special thanks to Michael Spens at Academy Editions (who suggested that I write this book), his editorial colleagues Maggie Toy and Eleanor Duffy, and David Rosie who designed the book.

Cover: Arup Associates, Sussex Stand, Goodwood racecourse, UK
Page 2: Scott Tallon and Walker, canopy for Papal mass, Dublin

First published in Great Britain in 1996 by
ACADEMY EDITIONS
An imprint of

ACADEMY GROUP LTD
42 Leinster Gardens, London W2 3AN
Member of the VCH Publishing Group

ISBN 1 85490 440 X

Distributed to the trade in the United States of America by
NATIONAL BOOK NETWORK, INC
4720 Boston Way, Lanham, Maryland 20706

Printed and bound in Singapore

CONTENTS

SOFT CANOPIES

Compression

Tension

Bending

a   *b*   *c*

Structural components are most efficient in tension

1. The behaviour of slender components in compression, bending and tension

2. Minimalist structure

DEFINITIONS

Tension roofs or canopies are those in which every part of the structure is loaded only in tension, with no requirement to resist compression or bending forces.

Pure tension is by far the most efficient way of using a slender structural member. As the analogy of a walking stick will show, a structural member subjected to compression will fail at loads well below its ultimate strength by buckling (figure la) and one subjected to bending will do the same owing to the generation of internal stresses that are very high in relation to the applied load (figure lb). It would take, by comparison, a very high load indeed to break the same component if the force is applied in tension only (figure lc): in this case, uniquely, the member works up to the full tensile strength of its material.

Tension structures are therefore very appropriate when the designer wishes to use the minimum amount of material either for functional reasons or, more commonly, for aesthetic ones. Seeing a structure in which every part is working to maximum efficiency can be a source of pleasure and excitement – as we know from instances as different as a suspension bridge (figure 2), hang-glider, or the sails and rigging of a yacht. There are three basic types of tension roof:

- Fabric roofs or canopies (figure 3). These are thin, flexible membranes held in shape by the application of tension, and acting simultaneously as structure and as weather shield.
- Cable net roofs (figure 4). In this case a structural net is held in tension, and carries a quite separate non-structural layer of weather-shielding elements such as acrylic glass sheets, wooden shingles, or the like.
- Pneumatic roofs. In this case a weather shield membrane is held aloft by air pressure (figure 5).

This book deals *only* with canopies of the first type, and *only* with those suspended in the open air. Complete fabric enclosures such as the Schlumberger Research

3-5. Tent, cable net and pneumatic structures (this book deals only with the first type)

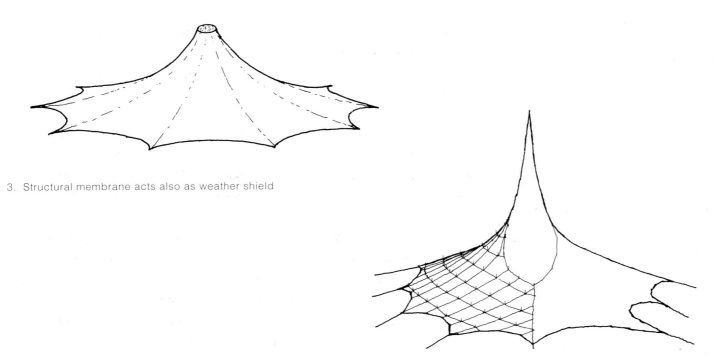

3. Structural membrane acts also as weather shield

4. Structural net carries separate non-structural weather shielding units

5. Weather shield membrane is supported by air pressure

Centre (figure 6) have special U-value and fire safety requirements and would benefit from separate coverage.

HISTORY

TRADITIONAL FABRIC STRUCTURES

In terms of architectural function the origins of the modern membrane roof lie in the traditional awning and tent, though in terms of structural performance and appearance the stressed surface of a nautical sail would be a closer analogy.

Awnings of substantial size and sophistication go back at least two thousand years. We know from pictorial representations and architectural remains that some Roman theatres and amphitheatres were fitted with *velaria* made of linen fabric. These were slung between fibre ropes and could be drawn across the central space to provide shade. More recently woven awnings known as 'toldos' have been used to provide shade over Spanish streets, and there are many other examples in hot climates.

Tents made of animal skins or woven materials have an even longer history and have been used all over the world, particularly in nomadic societies needing light, portable shelters. Examples of the latter include the native American tepee, the Mongolian yurt, and the Black Tent used by desert nomads of the Sahara, Arabia and Iran – these Bedouin tents are particularly impressive.

There was little development of Western tents between Roman times and the nineteenth century, perhaps partly because of lack of demand, and partly because of lack of advance in the strengths of cables, textiles and joints. But after the industrial revolution there evolved both a demand for large tents (used for mass entertainments such as circuses) and the availability of stronger materials, the latter mass-produced and relatively inexpensive. Impressive makes of tent were developed including the Chapiteau and Stromeyer brands which had diameters of up to 50 metres, complex geometries, and were fabricated from machine woven linen or hemp canvas.

TWENTIETH-CENTURY INNOVATIONS

In all the above examples the membranes were relatively slack and stability was derived from a combination of guy ropes, self-weight and the inherent stiffness of comparatively thick, heavy materials.

A new era opened after the second world war with the development of an

6. Fully enclosed tent structures, as distinct from canopies in the open air, are not covered in this book. Above is the Schlumberger Research Centre, Cambridge.

altogether novel type of fabric structure – light and flexible membranes held stable not by weight and stiffness but by designed-in curvature plus deliberately induced pre-stress which exploited the characteristics of new materials.

There were two prime innovators. Best known to architects is the architect and engineer Frei Otto who in 1957 founded the Centre for the Development of Lightweight Construction in Berlin, followed in 1964 by his more famous Institute for Lightweight Structures at Stuttgart University. His companion was Peter Stromeyer, whose family firm has been one of Europe's foremost manufacturers of very large tents since 1872.

Otto started experimenting with lightweight form by making and testing scale models with materials such as soap bubbles, nets and elastic membranes which he used in tension only. One of his earliest realised projects was the simple but delightful little music pavilion at the Federal Garden Exhibition at Kassel, Germany, in 1955 (figure 7).

From Kassel flowed a generation of German open air canopies for garden shows, trade shows and national exhibitions, which introduced a succession of new ideas about shape, erection technique, stressing method, materials and jointing.

These structures, many of them temporary, had a potent and invigorating influence on the subsequent course of architecture. They offered a combination of structural clarity and aesthetic appeal, the billowing forms often recalling natural phenomena such as waves, clouds or snow-capped mountain tops, that came as a source of inspiration to several generations of designers searching for architectural form based on fundamental principle rather than fashion.

The cloths and coatings available to Frei Otto in the 1950s allowed only very limited spans and life expectancies. Today, as a result of advances in textile technology, there are built examples of impressive size (see figure 8), excellent fire resistance and with life expectancies of twenty-five years or more. The fabric roof, an ancient method of shelter that unfortunately never became part of the classical canon of forms, is finally beginning to take its place in the normal architectural vocabulary.

APPROPRIATE USE

Stressed fabric canopies may be chosen in preference to alternative forms of structure (most of which may well be cheaper) for any of the following reasons:

• Their light and airy appearance. Most people walking past Lord's Cricket Ground

7. The pioneering 1955 music pavilion at Kassel, Germany

8. Hajj Terminal, Jeddah, Saudi Arabia

in London, whether they are aficionados of modern design or not, find their spirits lifted by the gleaming white tent tops floating unobtrusively above the curved facade (figure 9).

- Symbolic evocation. The tent roofs at Lord's Cricket Ground deliberately recall the marquee tents round an English village green, and there are many examples in Saudi Arabia and adjacent areas which recall desert tents or Islamic architectural forms.

- Translucency. The space beneath a fabric canopy can be bathed in a pleasant diffused light; the Mound Stand at Lord's Cricket Ground, again suceeds in this respect.

- Cost. Because of the high loads that must be collected and taken out into the surrounding building structure by cables and other devices, tensioned fabric canopies are not normally particularly low-cost. But they may be fully cost-effective where foldability, demountability and/or portability is an important requirement. Three such examples are shown at the end of this book – the folding umbrellas in the Prophet's Holy Mosque at Madinah; the demountable Buckingham Palace Ticket Office in London, which is required for only two months every year and then put in storage; and the mobile Carlos Moseley Pavilion in New York, which is carried on five trucks and can be set up on any stretch of grass in under six hours to form a sophisticated performance venue for music.

Arising from these characteristics, suitable applications for stressed fabric canopies could include:

- The shading of large open air spaces in hot climates. Examples are the Hajj Terminal in Saudi Arabia (figure 8) and the Yulara International Tourist Resort in Northern Territory, Australia (figure 10).

- The roofing of open air performance or exhibition spaces, such as Il Grande Bigo on Genoa Waterfront, Italy (figure 11).

- The roofing of sports stadia. British examples include the already-mentioned Mound Stand at Lord's Cricket Ground and Sussex Stand at Goodwood Racecourse (figure 12), which must give protection against both sun and rain. An Italian example is the Bari Stadium (figure 13) which in view of the local climate is required only to provide sun shading.

- Shelters over entrances or walkways. There are countless such canopies all over the world. An elegant example from Le Grand Bleu in Marseilles, France, (Regional Centre of Government, Les Bouches-du-Rhone) is illustrated here (figure 14).

9. Mound Stand, Lord's Cricket Ground, London

10. Yulara Tourist Resort, Ayers Rock, Australia

12. Sussex Stand, Goodwood Racecourse, UK

11. Il Grande Bigo, Genoa, Italy

13. San Nicola Stadium, Bari, Italy

14. Le Grand Bleu, Marseilles, France

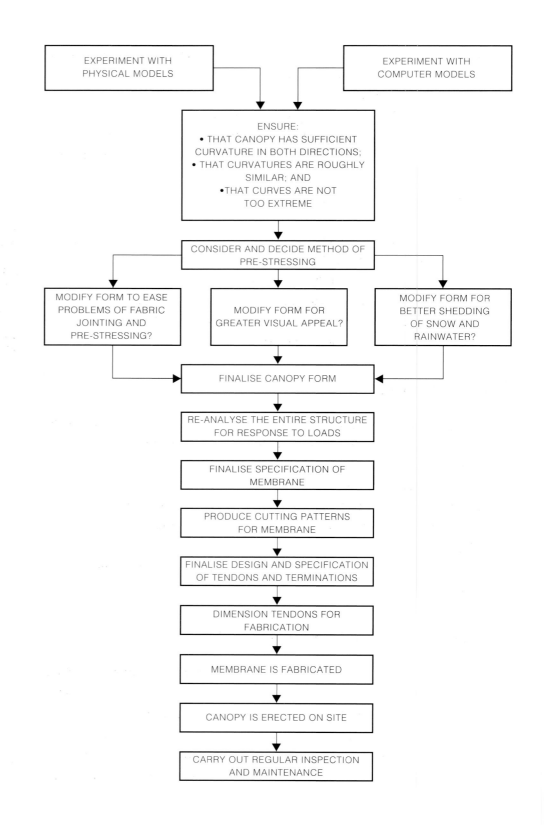

```
┌─────────────────────┐                    ┌─────────────────────┐
│ EXPERIMENT WITH     │                    │ EXPERIMENT WITH     │
│ PHYSICAL MODELS     │                    │ COMPUTER MODELS     │
└─────────────────────┘                    └─────────────────────┘
```

ENSURE:
• THAT CANOPY HAS SUFFICIENT
CURVATURE IN BOTH DIRECTIONS;
• THAT CURVATURES ARE ROUGHLY
SIMILAR; AND
• THAT CURVES ARE NOT
TOO EXTREME

CONSIDER AND DECIDE METHOD OF
PRE-STRESSING

MODIFY FORM TO EASE
PROBLEMS OF FABRIC
JOINTING AND
PRE-STRESSING?

MODIFY FORM FOR
GREATER VISUAL APPEAL?

MODIFY FORM FOR
BETTER SHEDDING
OF SNOW AND
RAINWATER?

FINALISE CANOPY FORM

RE-ANALYSE THE ENTIRE STRUCTURE
FOR RESPONSE TO LOADS

FINALISE SPECIFICATION OF
MEMBRANE

PRODUCE CUTTING PATTERNS
FOR MEMBRANE

FINALISE DESIGN AND SPECIFICATION
OF TENDONS AND TERMINATIONS

DIMENSION TENDONS FOR
FABRICATION

MEMBRANE IS FABRICATED

CANOPY IS ERECTED ON SITE

CARRY OUT REGULAR INSPECTION
AND MAINTENANCE

15. Stages of the design process

- Temporary, short-life shelters required only for a particular event and then destroyed. Examples include the umbrellas for Pink Floyd's 1978 tour of the USA (figure 16) and the Papal Canopies that were created specially for the Pope's visits to Bamberg, Dublin and Regensburg.
- Demountable shelters required for part of the year and kept in storage for the rest – for instance the already-mentioned Buckingham Palace Ticket Office.

APPROPRIATE FORM AND MATERIAL

In terms of *geometric form* a soft canopy must be curved in two opposite directions, a common configuration being the 'saddle-form' shown in figure 17 with its highly effective combination of concavity and convexity.

In terms of *material* most canopies are currently made either from polyvinyl chloride (PVC) coated polyester or polytetrafluorethylene (PTFE) coated glass. Both of these points are expanded and clarified below.

16. Pink Floyd umbrellas for their USA tour in 1978

DESIGN PROCESS

While design cannot be reduced to a strict linear process it is helpful to see the design of a fabric roof or canopy as a sequence of five broad stages:
- Evolving a suitable form
- Deciding a workable pre-stressing method
- Testing the proposed structure for stability under all loading conditions
- Dimensioning the parts (fabric and cables) for manufacture
- Finalising choice of materials and finishes.

These design stages are summarised in figure 15 and below each stage is looked at in turn.

DECIDING THE SURFACE GEOMETRY

The only practical way of making a thin, flexible membrane sufficiently stiff and flutter-proof to function as a roof or canopy is by a combination of *curvature* and *pre-stressing*. The deliberately induced curvature enables the membrane to transmit lateral loads which it could not do when flat, and the purpose of the pre-stress is to ensure that the fabric remains in tension, and therefore stable, even after the application of non-uniform loads such as wind buffeting or uplift. The pre-stress

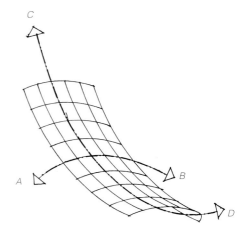

17. The doubly-curved saddle-shape typical of stressed fabric structures

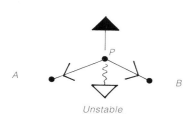

Unstable

A *B*

Unstable

18a,b and c. How a point P is stabilised against forces from all directions if restrained by two tension members A-B and C-D acting in opposing directions

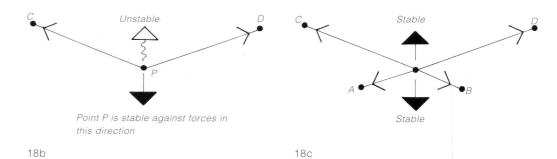

C *Unstable* *D*

P

Point P is stable against forces in this direction

18b

C *Stable* *D*

A *B*

Stable

18c

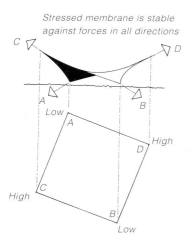

Stressed membrane is stable against forces in all directions

C *D*

A *B*

Low

A

D *High*

High *C*

B

High

Low

19. When many points restrained, as in figure 18, combine to form a surface, the whole surface will be stable against external forces

must be high enough (usually about half a tonne per metre width of fabric) never to be reduced to zero by opposite external forces.

The curvature must be of the right kind, and the sequence of diagrams in figure 18 illustrates the simple notion that underlies the complex mathematics of membrane design. If a point P is restrained by tension members anchored at A and B, that point will obviously be held stable against upward forces but will be unable to resist downward forces. Conversely, a point P that is restrained by tension members anchored at C and D will be held stable against downward forces but not upward ones. And a point that is restrained by two opposed sets of tension members APB and CPD will be stable against forces from all directions, as an inspection of the diagram will show.

If a soft membrane is simultaneously curved in two *opposed* directions A-B and C-D as shown in figure 19, and held in that shape by the application of pre-stress, then each individual point on its surface represents the condition shown in figure 18c and is stable against all external forces. If each individual point on the surface is stable against external forces then the entire surface must be similarly stable – and once this simple principle is grasped the ordinary designer will have the key to understanding even the most complex tensioned membrane forms.

The key concept is that of double curvature – but for this principle to work the two curvatures must be in opposed directions. Any area on the inner, shaded half of the torus shown in figure 20a would satisfy this principle, the curves A-B and C-D being in opposite directions (anticlastic). Conversely, while the dome shown in figure 20b is doubly-curved, the lines A-B and C-D both curve in the same direction and a fabric structure of this shape (synclastic) could only offer resistance to forces operating 'outwards' from the dome interior, not to ones operating 'inward' such as gravity or wind. It would not work. The same would apply to any area taken from the outer, unshaded half of figure 20a.

Figure 17 shows a typical saddle-shaped or 'anticlastic' shape. Lines A-B and C-D show the two opposed directions of curvature, one concave and one convex. Upward suction loads caused by wind are normally resisted by the membrane's tensile strength in the direction A-B (convex), and downward gravity loads from snow etcetera, by tensile strength in the direction C-D (concave). It will be seen that each of the canopy shapes shown later satisfies this principle.

The following points must be borne in mind when establishing the precise geometry of curvature:

- The more curved the surface, the more effective will be the pre-stress as a means of providing surface stiffness and preventing flutter.
- But against that, excessive curvature can make for practical difficulties in pre-stressing, particularly with stiff materials such as PTFE-coated glass fabric which resist deformation and do not allow the fabric to redistribute local overstressing.
- Rates of curvature across the canopy should be relatively uniform. Large variations can lead to soft areas in some places and stiff areas in others which is very undesirable.

Because the form of a tensioned membrane flows directly from the geometry of the boundaries between which it is stretched, the designer cannot simply sketch a shape and leave it to specialist engineers to 'make it happen'. In collaboration with his consultants he must design a boundary shape (walls, beams or cables) from which the kind of canopy shape he wants may be generated, and this process is described in the text on 'modelling' below. Such a boundary need not be flat but it must be continuous and without breaks of any kind.

Good design requires infinite care including the making of models (perhaps many models) which may be studied to ensure that there is a satisfactory architectural relationship between the fabric shape and its supporting structure. Too many fabric roofs show an unresolved relationship between the light and curvaceous canopy and the rectilinear building to which the canopy is fixed. Other membrane canopies, though elegant in themselves, have been spoilt by over-assertive struts and cabling systems.

Having made these preliminary points we can turn to the mechanics of stressed membrane form-finding. There are basically two methods, physical modelling and computer calculation.

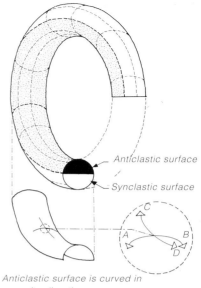

Anticlastic surface

Synclastic surface

Anticlastic surface is curved in opposite directions

20a. Anticlastic and synclastic surfaces

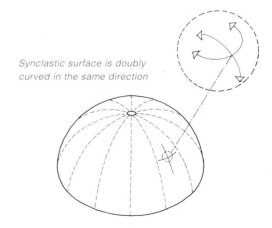

Synclastic surface is doubly curved in the same direction

20b. Synclastic surface

PHYSICAL MODELLING

The correct shape for a stressed fabric canopy can readily be found by physical modelling. Models may use either soap film or a thin textile such as nylon stocking material, lycra or heat-shrinkable PVC foil.

A soap film can be formed within a wire frame representing almost any desired set of boundaries. The film will automatically adopt a shape with uniform surface tension, and this will accurately define the geometry of the full-sized membrane. Photographs can therefore be taken of the film shape, measurements made, and the dimensions suitably scaled up to create the full-scale design. Alternatively nylon or some other thin textile material can be stretched over wire frames, possibly with attached weights, to mimic at small scale the proposed canopy.

Working with such models fosters a useful understanding of underlying structural principles but has the disadvantage that the scaling-up of the design from a very small original may lead also to the scaling-up of measurement errors and a seriously flawed final result.

COMPUTATION

There is an alternative method of form-finding: computer analysis, and many specialist design firms now have programmes giving highly reliable and accurate fabric shapes in response to stated design parameters. Two stages are involved:

- First the computer finds a form that a 'pure' membrane would assume if stretched between the proposed boundaries with uniform tension in all directions. In figure 21 the form is that of a soap film held between a rectangular outer boundary and a smaller inner ring, with the central ring pulled up to a higher level. For the purposes of analysis the surface ('field') is divided into small straight-edged triangles fitting in with the proposed radial layout of the strips of material from which the membrane will be fabricated (see the dotted area on figure 21a).
- Then the physical characteristics of the proposed membrane material are fed in and these inevitably produce a slightly modified form – taking into account, for instance, whether the woven material is more stretchy along its weft than its warp.

At all stages the designer has the facility of pushing and pulling the displayed forms about and changing them in all sorts of ways until a satisfactory solution is reached – testing alternative support positions; different boundary shapes; different

21. Simplified illustration of computer-aided form-finding and subsequent fine-tuning to give a shape that is functionally and aesthetically satisfactory. Canopy for Papal Mass, Dublin, Ireland. 21a shows the overall field divided into small straight-edged triangles for the purpose of computer analysis.

ways of collecting the surface tensions into cables and transferring these through the structure into the ground; and different types of membrane. The display can use colours to show how highly stressed the various parts of the structure are, and whether any parts of the membrane are not in tension (which, of course, is not acceptable).

Computer aided design is now extremely powerful but has disadvantages. One is that the designer may achieve correct answers without necessarily having any clear understanding of underlying physical principles. The other is that even the best computer image gives a less realistic understanding of shape than an accurate physical model. For instance, relatively flat horizontal areas may seem on a computer diagram to be sufficiently curved to disperse snow loads or rainwater (see below) when in fact they are not, as a physical model would easily show.

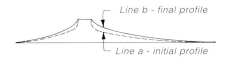

21b. Modifying the original profile

COMBINATION OF METHODS

The best approach may therefore be to use physical modelling for preliminary form-finding and visual form-testing; and computer analysis for precisely determining the final shape, validating it for stability under all loading conditions and generating the fabric-cutting patterns. The latter must be extremely accurate (figure 37).

FINE-TUNING THE THEORETICALLY-DERIVED SHAPE

Forms found by small-scale model or computer calculation may satisfactorily resolve all structural stresses, but there may still be practical reasons for wanting to modify the shape thus established. These could include:

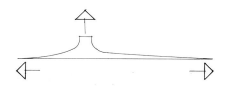

21c. Methods of creating pre-stress

- Snow load dispersal. In cold climates a mass of snow may slide down the steeper sections of a fabric canopy and settle on the flatter areas, causing a deep deflection. This deflection may then become a water-filled pond which sags even deeper as more meltwater flows in, leading ultimately to membrane failure. For this reason horizontal flat areas should be avoided or, alternatively, drained by means of grommets inserted in the fabric.
- Rainwater dispersal. Again it should be considered whether ponding may occur on the theoretically-derived shape.
- Appearance. The theoretically-derived form may not 'look right' and repeated modification may be required, possibly using large-scale physical models, to create a right-looking profile.
- Practical problems such as jointing or pre-stressing, particularly in areas of sharp curvature.

Figure 21b illustrates the last two points. The architects Scott Tallon and Walker

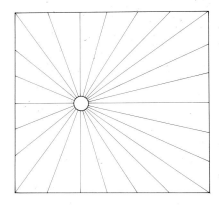

21d. Radial pattern of seams

envisaged the canopy as a square-based cone rising to a central ring, and a theoretically correct profile was easily found (line *a*). But a built prototype showed that it would be difficult to weld the seams at the sharply curved neck; pre-stressing studies also revealed practical problems at this point; and the architects felt that the shape anyway did not look quite right. An improved profile was evolved, as shown by line *b*, which solved all three of these problems.

In the case of large structures or canopies which may be subjected to unusual stress a full-scale model may be needed to test and verify structural behaviour, as was the case with the vast Hajj canopy in Saudi Arabia. This structure was designed by SOM to consist of over two hundred 45 x 45 metre conical fabric tents suspended from 45 metre high columns (figure 22). Two test units, an interior tent and a corner tent, were built in Ohio in 1978; hundreds of strain gauges, strain sensors and load cells were attached to fabric, cables and upper rings; and a $2.5 million test programme was run to verify the original computer analysis and to demonstrate the constructability of the roof system with its numerous connection details.

EDGE CONDITIONS

Any tensioned fabric roof must have a continuous boundary. This need not be flat but it must be without breaks of any kind – as can be demonstrated by a soap film, which will instantly rupture if there is any break in the frame within which it is held.

This boundary will help define the shape of the canopy, and will provide the locations where the loads are taken out of the membrane and transferred to the rigid structure. The boundary may be flexible or rigid. Where a straight edge is wanted the solution is a rigid 'bolt-rope' edge either bolted to an edge beam by means of clamp plates or sliding into an aluminium extrusion.

But most canopy edges are flexible, formed by a perimeter cable or belt in a continuous edge pocket (figure 23) or running outside the membrane and connected to it by loops as seen in figure 40. The canopy edge takes the form of a series of catenary curves giving a scalloped shape to the membrane and the perimeter cable or belt is collected at intervals by links to the major anchorage points as shown in figure 23. At these points the loads are taken out of the membrane and back to the surrounding structure. There are two important matters to bear in mind here:

- The shallower the perimeter curve the higher must be the tension in the perimeter cable and, therefore, in the anchorages holding that cable. Very high tensions can add greatly to costs and may require unpleasantly heavy-looking restraining systems.

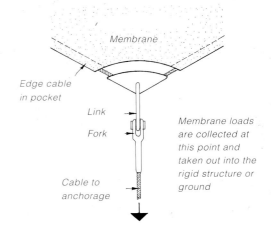

23. Typical edge cable detail at one of the perimeter locations where stresses are taken out of a membrane into the surrounding structure

Opposite: 22. Hajj Terminal, Jeddah, Saudi Arabia

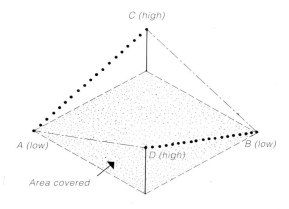

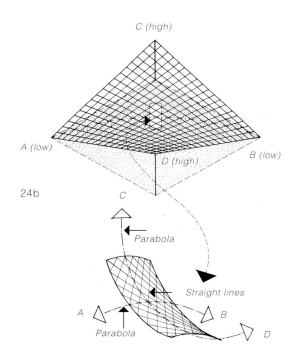

24a, b, c. How a hyperbolic paraboloid is formed, and the resultant surface configuration

24b

24c

- Perimeter connection points require exceptionally careful attention to movement, fabric reinforcement and the like if the membrane is not to wrinkle or tear. Expert advice is essential.

COMMON CANOPY SHAPES

There are two families of 'pure' anticlastic forms, hyperbolic paraboloids and double-ring shapes, examples of which are shown in figures 25 and 26. These ideal forms (in which the membrane tension is uniform in all directions and surface area is minimal, just as in a soap film) can then be modified by introducing peaks, humps or ridges into the geometric 'field' as shown in figures 27 to 29. In the latter cases the membrane will no longer be uniformly stressed and may require the incorporation of cables or fabric reinforcement at points of concentrated stress. These forms cannot be modelled by soap film (which would instantly rupture if distorted in this way) but can be represented by stretched fabric models.

Hyperbolic paraboloids (hypars): This is a simple and attractive canopy shape, generated between two low and two high points as already shown in figure 19. If a straight line is moved from the position A-C to D-B in such a manner that its ends move along straight lines A-D and C-B (figure 24a), the resultant saddle-shaped form will have four straight boundaries while A-B and C-D will each be a parabola. As shown in figure 24c these parabolas will be of opposite curvatures, A-B being convex and C-D concave just as required by the principles of double-curvature described on page 14. Using tensile strength only, membrane fibres in the direction A-B will be able to resist wind uplift while those in the direction C-D will be able to resist gravity loads, and overall the membrane will be held stable against all applied loads (provided, of course, there is sufficient pre-stress).

Hypars are often created by four boundary cables spanning between two masts forming the high points C and D, and two ground anchorages forming the low points A and B as shown in figure 7.

Double-ring forms (including cones): The shape generated between a large outer ring and a smaller inner ring, the latter lifted to form an apex, is another pure form (figure 26). The outer 'ring' could actually be rectangular as in figure 21. For membrane tension to be uniform, radius A-B must at every point be the same as radius C-D, which implies quite a large apex ring and a cone of very specific shape. Should the designer want a

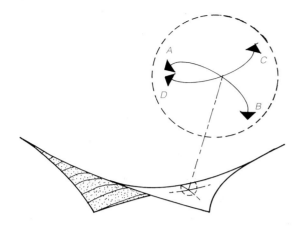

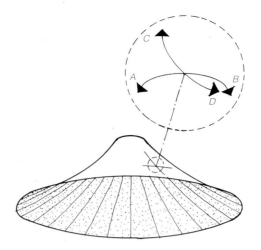

25, 26. Two basic anticlastic
shapes: the hyperbolic paraboloid
(25) and double-ring cone (26)

26.

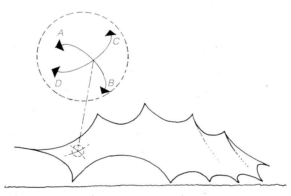

27, 28, 29. Modified shapes formed by
pushing or pulling the field into one or
more peaks (27), rounded humps (28) or
ridged humps (29)

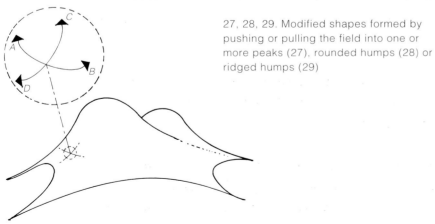

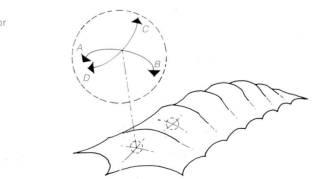

28.

29.

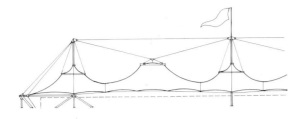

30.

31.

32.

30, 31, 32. Double-ring cones at the Mound Stand, London (30), relying on membrane strength only; and Pensacola pool, USA, with radial cables supporting the membrane (32). Figure 31 shows pointed cones at Goodwood racecourse

smaller apex ring or try to modify the cone profile by, for instance, pulling up the apex to a point where radius C-D becomes greater than radius A-B, a soap bubble would quickly burst, indicating that membrane stress was no longer uniform. In real life the canopy would therefore need reinforcement of some kind – in its weave, by additional layers of material, by using strong radial seams, or by inserting radial cables under the fabric as in figure 22, in which case chafing between cable and membrane must be allowed for.

One example of a double-ring form is the Mound Stand at Lord's Cricket Ground in London (figure 30). An additional fabric cone has in some cases been formed above the upper ring as shown in the figure. This provides rain-proofing and also gives a more satisfying shape than the 'truncated cone' that would otherwise result. The Mound Stand roofs are generally held to exemplify soft canopy design at its most excellent. The Sussex Stand at Goodwood racecourse is another handsome example (see cover).

Examples of cone-shaped membranes resting on radial cables include the pool covering at Pensacola in the USA (figure 32) and in Britain the Bath Panorama tent and Liverpool Garden Festival tent.

Pointed forms: Sharply pointed shapes (figure 27) can be very attractive but a true membrane cannot be supported by a point, as can be shown by trying to support a soap film by a needle – the concentration of forces will cause an instant rupture. Some method must be found for dealing with the concentrated stress at each peak. One approach is to incorporate a number of ridge cables at the mast point to transfer the uniform stress in the fabric to the concentrated load at the mast, while in smaller examples local fabric reinforcement in the form of a circular apex clamp may be enough (figure 33). Examples of pointed canopies include the Edinburgh Ross Bandstand Tent in Scotland and the row of smaller canopies at Goodwood racecourse (figure 31).

Round-humped forms: Again these are forms (figure 28) which cannot be modelled by soap film and in which membrane tension is not uniform. Specific areas of membrane within the 'field' are pushed up by umbrella-shaped frames, and the fabric distorts into a doubly-curved surface over each such domed support by weave rearrangement. Examples include the British Genius Exhibition Tent at Battersea Park and the Imagination headquarters, both in London. The latter, part-sketched in figure 35, is not strictly speaking a canopy but the roof of an enclosed building, however it offers a good example of the form. Figure 34 shows the push-up umbrella ensemble that forms the domed shape in the membrane.

Ridge-humped forms: If the ridge occurs *within* a field then this is a variation of the type described above but using a linear arch as a local support rather than a rounded dome (figure 29). An example is the Buckingham Palace Ticket Office in London. Here the ridges are formed from above rather than below, by clamping the membrane joints between coat hanger-shaped plates suspended from an overhead ridge cable (see page 49).

If the ridges form the boundaries *between* adjacent membrane fields as in figure 11, rather than occurring within an individual field, then each field can of course be a pure shape of uniform stress and minimal area as modelled by a soap film.

DECIDING A WORKABLE PRE-STRESSING METHOD

It is essential to make a design which is capable in practice of being pre-stressed. There are three practical matters to be considered – membrane shape, membrane material, and support systems.

MEMBRANE SHAPE
Excessive curvature of the fabric can create stressing difficulties and expert advice must be taken before membrane form is finalised. Figure 21b gives an example of the kind of modifying process that may be required.

MEMBRANE MATERIAL
Practical problems are greater with PTFE-coated glass fabric (which is too stiff to allow the fabric to redistribute local overstressing) than with PVC-coated polyester (which, being more flexible and better able to redistribute stresses, is a more tolerant material).

SUPPORT SYSTEMS
The fabric must be held by a system of parts that can be sufficiently moved to create the necessary strains in the fabric. There are basically two ways of creating pre-stress:
- Laterally expanding the base;
- Pulling up (or pushing up) the apex.

These principles can be seen in figure 21c where pre-stress could be induced either by pushing the base diameter outwards, or by raising the central disc, or by some combination of the two. Finding the best way in any particular case involves

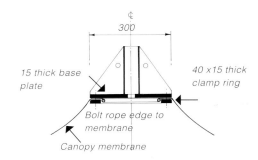

33. Clamp ring detail at the apex of pointed-cone canopy at Bath Football Club stadium

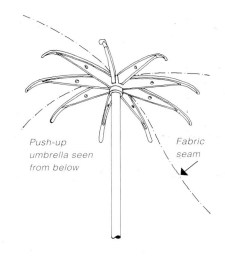

34. A round-humped roof: the Imagination Headquarters in London by Herron Associates

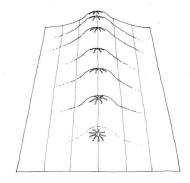

35. Round-humped membrane seen from above

much calculation and testing, perhaps using physical models.

The necessary movement is normally created by rotating threaded bars or fittings in order to shorten overall tendon length. Typical fittings are shown in figure 41.

DECIDING WEAVE AND SEAM DIRECTIONS

Having established the canopy profile and the movements by which the fabric will be pre-stressed, care must now be taken that weave directions and seam layouts are correctly oriented in relation to the main directions of curvature and the directions of pre-stress. Two matters are important:

- Appearance. Membrane canopies are made up from strips of fabric and the joints between these will form a prominent pattern. The direction and layout of the seams are therefore not just a technical problem but a vital aspect of the visual design. In figure 21d the radial pattern of seams sweeping up to the central disc adds greatly to the grace and expressiveness of the canopy. Radial patterns are usual with conic shapes.
- Crimp interchange. Woven fabrics are normally tensioned in the 'weft' (or 'fill') direction rather than the 'warp' direction for a reason explained in figure 36b. If tension is applied in direction A as shown in figure 36a, the fabric is pre-stressed only along the axis A. But if tension is applied in direction B the weft fibres partly straighten out, and in so doing transfer a proportion of their crimp to the warp fibres, thus shortening the latter. In this case tensioning only in one direction (axis B) therefore creates pre-stress along both axes A and B, a useful phenomenon.

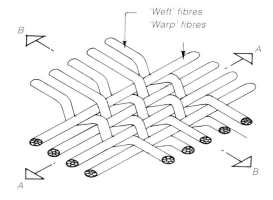

'Weft' fibres
'Warp' fibres

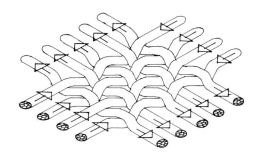

36a, b. The useful phenomenon of crimp interchange

ANALYSING THE STRUCTURE'S RESPONSE TO LOADS

Having achieved a provisional design, computer analysis must be carried out to check that the chosen form and fabric really can cope with the complex forces that are generated by pre-stressing and external loads. Such calculations need special expertise and should be carried out by experienced consultants – see Appendix A.

DIMENSIONING THE PARTS FOR FABRICATION

The final design stage involves working out the precise fabric cutting patterns for manufacture. This is normally done as part of the process described in the section above and by the same consultancy. The aim is a set of parts (like the parts of a dress) that:

- Can be cut from rolls of textile of standard width without waste of material.
- Can be fitted together to neatly form the doubly curved shapes established in the section above.
- Will allow correct weave directions and positioning of seams in relation to pre-stress.

Dimensions must be precise, and so also the tolerances at all critical points. Figure 37 (overleaf) shows an example taken from the case study on pages 48-53.

THE FABRICATION AND ERECTION PROCESS

Fairly minor fabrication and/or construction errors (for instance, a membrane that is slightly too small or a supporting frame that is slightly too large) may lead to inaccurate pre-stressing. Most canopies cannot be pre-assembled in the workshop for testing: the fitting together of perhaps hundreds of parts on site is both the first and the last opportunity for discovering mistakes. It is essential to involve experienced designers and manufacturers – see Appendix A.

FABRIC CHOICE AND SPECIFICATION

FABRIC TYPES

Having outlined the design process (surface geometry, pre-stressing method, and the dimensioning of parts) we must turn our attention more closely to the actual materials used to form soft canopies. There are three basic textile types: woven fabrics, films and reinforced films. Because woven fabrics are the most commonly used we describe these in some detail and give only brief notes on films and reinforced films.

Woven fabrics: These are woven from yarns set at right angles to each other. The yarns stretched along the length of the cloth during weaving are known as the 'warp' and those threaded through across the width of the cloth, at lower tension, as the 'weft', as shown in figure 36a. Woven fabrics are normally anisotropic (they behave differently along the directions of warp and weft), though these differences can be minimised or eliminated by weaving and coating technique.

BUCKINGHAM PALACE TICKET OFFICE Panel 1 + 2

SIDE 1				SIDE 2		
LENGTH (Y)	OFFSET (X)	NODE		LENGTH (Y)	OFFSET (X)	NODE
2.707	0.359	405		2.707	0.359	405
2.746	0.191	404		2.690	0.444	406
2.792	0.024	18 *		2.676	0.530	407 *
2.457	0.156	403		2.385	0.520	577
2.109	0.251	402		2.093	0.511	576
1.753	0.307	401		1.801	0.501	575
1.393	0.324	400		1.509	0.492	574
1.034	0.301	399		1.217	0.483	573
0.679	0.239	398		0.925	0.475	572
0.333	0.138	397		0.633	0.466	571
0.000	0.000	17 *		0.340	0.458	570
0.039	0.359	361		0.048	0.449	362 *
				0.039	0.359	361

(diagram with nodes: Y axis, 18, 404, 405 406 407, 407, 403, 577, 402, 576, 401, 575, 400, 574, 399, 573, 398, 572, 397, 571, 570, 362, 17, 361, X axis)

COMPENSATION	Warp%	Fill%
End 2	0.46	0.65
End 1	0.46	0.65

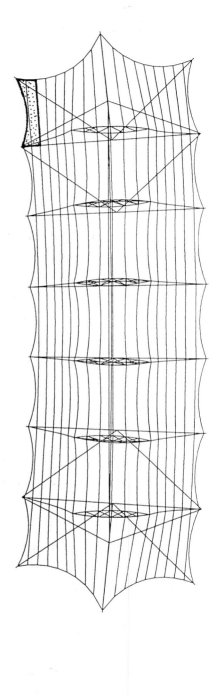

37. Example of a fabric cutting pattern: the Buckingham Palace ticket office in London by Sir Michael Hopkins and Partners (see pages 48-53)

Most soft canopies are made of PVC-coated polyester or PTFE-coated glass fibre. PVC-coated polyester is easier to work and is cheaper in first cost than PTFE-coated glass fibre, but it is also less durable, requires more frequent cleaning, and stretches more under load. Table 1 summarises the key characteristics (see page 29).

Films: These are thin homogenous sheets of plastic or rubber. They can be completely transparent or completely opaque, are highly flexible, and are normally isotropic (ie behave in the same way both along the length and breadth of any given sheet). But they are weaker, less durable and less tear-resistant than woven fabrics. They are most appropriate for temporary canopies or ephemeral constructions such as rock concert venues where their high flexibility and low cost are advantageous.

Reinforced films: These consist of a woven fabric glued or heat-welded between two thin layers of film. Laminates of this kind offer the strength and permanence of woven fabrics combined with the impermeability of films. A high degree of translucency may be obtained by using an open-weave core fabric plus translucent film. They would be suitable for more permanent structures than those mentioned under 'films'.

FABRIC CHARACTERISTICS

There are three categories of performance that are of interest to the designer:
- Short-term structural properties (determined mainly by the membrane material but also influenced, in the case of coated woven cloths, by the coating).
- Long-term structural properties (how the above properties are maintained over time and under cyclic loading)
- Non-structural properties (eg translucency, cleanability and resistance to fading or discoloration).

The key *short-term* structural properties are:

Tensile strength: Tensile strength, or resistance to failure under load, must be high enough to enable the fabric to bear the loads required of it. Both PVC-coated polyester and PTFE-coated glassfibre can be produced with strengths of up to 16 tonnes per metre width.

Tensile modulus: The higher the modulus (resistance to stretching) the more the cloth will resist being moulded to the prescribed canopy profiles and the more critical will be complete accuracy of cutting and installation. Woven polyester fabrics have a medium modulus, are easy to use, and their relative 'stretchiness' is normally not a problem from a structural point of view except where large snow loads are expected. Woven glass fabrics have a high modulus and may carry a risk of wrinkles, creases and sags if the cloth does not exactly fit the profiles on site.

Tear strength: Tensioned fabric roofs are more likely to fail by tearing than by direct tensile failure, therefore tear strength and resistance to tear propagation are vitally important. PVC-coated polyester has medium tear resistance and PTFE-coated glass cloth has a high tear resistance. Reinforced films have lower tear strengths than either of these and films the lowest of all.

Directionality: The issue here is whether the fabric behaves similarly in all directions (isotropic) or differently in different directions (anisotropic). Woven fabrics are traditionally anisotropic, being stiffer in the 'warp' direction than the 'weft', but it is becoming possible to reduce or even eliminate such directionality by modern weaving and coating techniques if this is desired. Non-woven films are isotropic.

The key *long-term* structural properties are:

Construction stretch: All woven fabrics undergo some non-recoverable construction stretch as the crimp is pulled out (figure 36b) during construction. The degree of stretch will be much greater in the weft direction than the warp and these figures must be known so that appropriate compensation can be made in the cutting patterns. This data must be obtained from the cloth manufacturer.

Dimensional stability: For woven fabrics the dimensional stability (resistance to creep, thermal movement and moisture movement) under long term loading depends more on the basic material than on the type of weave or coating, though both of the latter will have an influence.

Such movement is undesirable in permanently stressed structures since they cause loss of pre-stress. Polyester fabrics are relatively stable in terms of thermal

Table 1 Properties of the two fabrics most commonly used for soft canopies

Property	Fabric PVC-coated polyester	PTFE-coated glass
1. Short-term structural properties:		
Tensile strength	Medium	High
Tensile modulus	Medium	High
Tear strength	Medium	High
Directionality	Normally stiffer in the warp direction than the weft but there are fabrics available with virtually identical properties in both directions	As for PVC-coated polyester
2. Long-term structural properties:		
Construction stretch	Medium	Low
Dimensional stability	Medium	High
3. Non-structural properties:		
Durability	Lifetime normally 10 to 12 years depending on (a) exposure and (b) opacity of coating. Design life could be only 3 to 5 years with highly translucent coatings and up to to 15 years with opaque coatings. A white finish will reduce surface temperature and enhance durability	25 years or more
Translucency	8% to 30%	5% to 15%
Appearance	All colours available. Can be opaque or translucent. Suffers from dirt retention so that visual rather than physical deterioration is likely to determine working life	White and a few other colours are available. Dirt is not retained and surface remains clean. No discoloration
4. Ease of installation:		
Flexibility	High, making for easy fabrication, transportation and installation	Low, creating a risk of damage during fabrication, transportation and installation. Accurate cutting and installation vital.
Jointing	Easily done	Specialist techniques needed
5. Summary comments:		
	Overall the most popular coated fabric, and there are many experienced installers. Cheap enough to be replaced every 10 years to maintain pristine appearance	Used for canopies where long life and/or low maintenance are more important than low cost or ease of installation

and moisture movement but the creep is such that half the pre-stress may be lost in the first ten days, a further half over the next hundred, and a further half over the next thousand, so that re-stressing may be necessary after a period. Glass fabrics, by contrast, have high dimensional stability.

The key *non-structural* properties are:

Durability: In woven fabrics, durability for a given degree of exposure depends mainly on the nature of the coating: the more opaque the coating the better-protected will be the fabric and the longer will be fabric life. PVC-coated fabrics may last only three to five years if translucency is 30 per cent but up to fifteen years with a translucency of 15 per cent. An average lifespan for PVC-coated fabrics would be ten to twelve years, and twenty years in favourable conditions. PTFE-coated fabrics may last thirty years.

Translucency: In woven fabrics translucency depends partly on the translucency of the yarn material, partly on the spacing of the yarns, partly on the translucency of the coating material, and all three can be varied to produce a desired result. PVC-coated polyester cloths may have translucencies of 8 to 30 per cent and PTFE-coated glass cloths from 5 to 15 per cent. In films translucency depends both on the basic material and the coating. Films are available ranging from almost 100 per cent transparency to complete opacity.

FABRIC JOINT SPECIFICATION

There are three principal methods for jointing woven fabrics:

SEWN JOINTS

These are the strongest type of joint but the thread is susceptible to degradation. Sewing is suitable for PVC-coated polyester where it is normally combined with heat sealing for maximum strength, and in external situations the joint should be protected by a PVC cover. Sewing is not suitable for PTFE-coated glass owing to the brittleness of the yarn.

HEAT WELDED JOINTS

Heat welding is done by heating the seam to above the melting point of the fabric and then letting it cool while applying pressure. The heating can be done by a jet

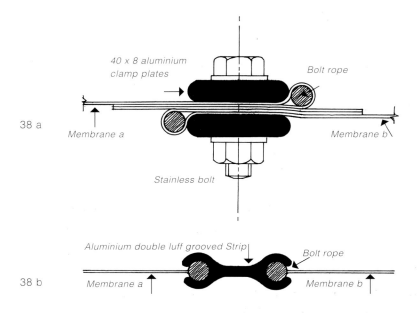

40 x 8 aluminium clamp plates

Bolt rope

Membrane a

Membrane b

Stainless bolt

Aluminium double luff grooved Strip

Bolt rope

Membrane a

Membrane b

of hot air, by contact with heated elements, or, most frequently, by radio-frequency electro-magnetic radiation.

Heat welded joints are suitable for both PVC-coated polyester and PTFE-coated glass fabric. In the latter case an interlayer of a different material must be used as the PTFE does not itself melt.

MECHANICAL JOINTS

Though they can be used on site, sewn and heat welded joints are best made in the workshop and some kind of mechanical jointing is often preferred for on-site execution. There are three common types.

- The roped edges of two sheets of fabric are clamped between plates as shown on figure 38a. The plates should be discontinuous to allow movement.
- The roped edges of two sheets of fabric are held in an extruded aluminium 'double luff grooved strip' as shown in figure 38b. Again the plates should be discontinuous. This method is less waterproof than the one above.
- The simplest method is to connect a series of shallow scallops at frequent intervals by means of shackles. This kind of joint is easily and quickly assembled on site but is not waterproof.

TENDON CHOICE AND SPECIFICATION

CHOICE OF TENDON TYPE

Where stiffness and corrosion resistance are overriding requirements, and

38a, b. Mechanical joints in a stressed membrane

especially in external situations where there is some doubt whether the client will carry out regular maintenance inspections, *solid rods* will normally be the most effective tendons.

Where flexibility, curving geometries and a high strength-to-weight ratio are important the choice will probably be a *spun cable*. But in that case, if the location is external and subject to rain, the designer should establish that the client understands the importance of regular cable inspection and maintenance.

Solid rods: High tensile steel tendons are available for use in soft canopies in diameters ranging from about 4 to 35 millimetres and can be subjected to higher loads than cables of the same diameter because of the absence of 'cable stretch'. But a rod may cost two and a half times as much as a 1 × 19 cable of the same capacity, and the most cost-effective solution may simply be to use a larger diameter cable.

Spun cables: Figure 39 shows four commonly used cable types. In terms of structural efficiency and corrosion resistance a compact strand 'Dyform' cable will give the best performance for a given diameter, a conventional cable spun from a few thick wires the next best, and one woven from many thin wires the worst. But from the point of view of flexibility the ranking is exactly the reverse, with a cable spun from many thin wires being most appropriate and the 'Dyform' cable least so. Common specifications would therefore be:

- In standard situations, conventional 1 x 19 strand cable. This is available in diameters ranging from about 3 millimetres (breaking load 0.7 tonnes) to 26 millimetres (breaking load 40 tonnes).

		Axial stiffness	Flexural stiffness	Tensile strength
●	High tensile rod	High	High	High
	1 x 19 'Dyform' compact strand	↕	↕	↕
	1 x 19 strand			
	7 x 19 strand	Low	Low	Low

39. Common types of spun cable

- Where high strength/low stretch are prime requirements, 1 x 19 compact strand ('Dyform') cable. This is available in diameters ranging from about 5 millimetres (breaking load 2.4 tonnes) to 19 millimetres (breaking load 31 tonnes).
- Where flexibility is a prime requirement, conventional 7 x 19 wire rope. This is available in diameters ranging from about 3 millimetres (breaking load 0.5 tonnes) to 12 millimetres (breaking load 8 tonnes).

CHOICE OF TENDON MATERIAL AND FINISH

Tendons are available in various steels as mentioned below. If stainless steel pins are combined with forks of other steels, as may be the case, then Tufnol isolating washers and bushes may be necessary to prevent bimetallic corrosion.

Solid rods: Where corrosion resistance and/or a bright appearance are prime requirements, stainless steel or Nitronic 50 steel are the obvious choices. A rod made from Nitronic 50 steel will be stronger, less stretchy and more expensive than one of equivalent diameter in stainless steel.

Where corrosion resistance is of lower priority, galvanised steel, painted and maintained in the ordinary way, will be cheaper in first cost than either of the above. Galvanised steel rods with threaded ends must be heavily coated with grease before being screwed into position, to protect the threaded ends (where the galvanising has been cut away) against corrosion.

Spun cables: Stainless steel cables have a handsome, bright appearance, are most expensive in first cost and usually require no further anti-corrosion treatment – though they may be vulnerable in corrosive atmospheres such as chlorinated swimming pools, and expert advice should be sought. Stainless steel cables can be PVC coated for additional protection or to give a desired appearance.

Galvanised steel cables are dull grey in appearance and cheaper in first cost than stainless steel, but also less corrosion resistant. In covered situations corrosion can usually be ignored but in the open air the galvanising will have a limited life, as will the protective grease packing with which such cables are normally supplied. For added resistance an external galvanised steel cable can be impregnated with zinc paste during the spinning process, which may give a life of up to fifty years, and/or sheathed. However sheathed cables may look unattractive, will carry the risk that incipient corrosion will be hidden and undetected, and are not recommended for external situations.

Cable tension: Cables are damaged more by cyclical loading and vibration (caused for example by wind) than by high steady loads. From this point of view a relatively high cable tension may be good rather than bad. Usual practice is to design to a safety factor of five so that the cable is loaded to 20 per cent of maximum breaking load.

Cable bending radius: If cables are curved too tightly they lose strength and may even come apart. The degree of risk varies between cable types and expert advice should be sought, but as a rule of thumb bending radius should be at least 500 times the diameter of the individual wire strands.

TENDON TERMINATIONS

Well designed terminations and junctions (figure 40) can add to the beauty of a canopy and ideally a coordinated family of fittings should be selected or designed to give a coherent appearance to a particular structure. If cables are used then proprietary rather than custom designed terminations are virtually obligatory. This presents no problem since excellently designed forks, eyes and adjustors are commercially available. See Appendix A for firms of repute.

The most commonly used fittings are illustrated in figure 41. The chosen method of termination will depend on:

- Whether the tendon is of fixed length or needs to be adjustable.
- What is considered the most convenient method of adjustment.
- Tendon length and diameter

FIXED-LENGTH TENDONS

Because tensile fabric structures are subject to much movement tendons must usually be of adjustable length. Where this is not so a solid rod can be used with each end swaged or welded to an eye or fork as shown in figure 41a. In these cases the pin-to-pin distance must be exactly specified as no substantial adjustment can be made on site. While a fixed-length tendon will usually be a solid rod rather than a cable, pre-stressing techniques may be used to remove the constructional stretch of a cable and enable it to be manufactured to a precise length.

ADJUSTABLE TENDONS

These are usual in tensile fabric structures and adjustment of length (for instance,

40. Tendon terminations at Il Grande Bigo, Genoa

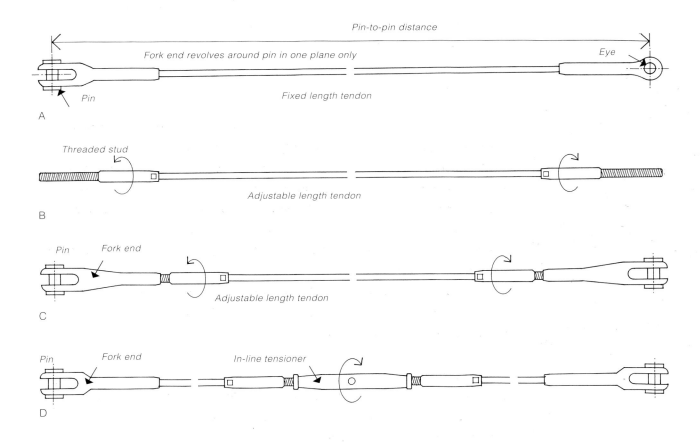

Pin-to-pin distance

Fork end revolves around pin in one plane only

Eye

Pin

Fixed length tendon

A

Threaded stud

Adjustable length tendon

B

Pin   Fork end

Adjustable length tendon

C

Pin   Fork end   In-line tensioner

D

41. Common methods of tendon adjustment

to tension a slack tendon) is always carried out by rotating a threaded component. If the connection between tendon and fork is not itself threaded (eg welded or swaged) then an additional threaded fitting may be required to provide such adjustability. Length adjustment may be done in two ways.

The first method of adjustment is by rotating a pair of *threaded studs* at the ends of the tendon. This is most appropriate for relatively short, rigid tendons. If the tendon does not need to accommodate in-plane movement, and is allowed to terminate in fixed anchorages, then figure 41b shows a suitable detail. Each end of the rod or cable terminates in a threaded stud, one with a left-hand thread and one right-hand, and each stud screws into some suitable form of anchorage such as a spigot. When the two studs are turned in one direction they are drawn into the spigots, tightening the tendon; when turned in the opposite direction tension is relaxed. This is an economical system.

If it is necessary for the tendon to move freely in one plane then figure 41c may apply. Each stud is screwed into a fork which in turn connects with the anchorage. Each fork can rotate around its pin, thus allowing the tendon to move as required in that plane. Again the tendon is tensioned by rotation of the studs. The system is symmetrical, aesthetically pleasing and fully adjustable.

The second method of adjustment is by rotating a *tensioner*, and this would be usual for long, flexible tendons. In this case both ends of the rod or cable terminate in forks which are anchored to the building. Somewhere along its length the tendon is divided, the two ends swaged to threaded studs with their threads in opposite directions, and these studs are screwed into the tensioner as shown in figure 41d. When the tensioner is turned in the appropriate direction the threaded studs are drawn in, tightening the tendon.

MOVEMENT IN TWO PLANES

Standard forks allow free movement in one plane (rotating about the pin) but not in two. This is satisfactory in a structure that has been specifically designed to exclude out-of-plane movements. But where out-of-plane movement may occur 'toggle forks' (figure 42) must be used to eliminate all risk of bending stresses being induced in tendons – because, to recall the very first words of this essay, tension structures are those 'in which every part of the structure is loaded only in tension, with no requirement to resist compression or bending forces'. It is absolutely essential that this condition be ensured throughout the whole structure and across all junctions.

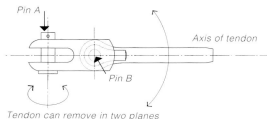

Pin A

Axis of tendon

Pin B

Tendon can remove in two planes

42. A 'toggle fork' that allows movement to occur in two planes without transmitting bending stresses

CONNECTION METHODS

The physical connection between the tendon, on the one hand, and the fork, eye or stud on the other, may be made by screw-thread, swaging or (in the case of solid rods only) welding.

Screwed connections provide some opportunity for adjustment but are more expensive than swaging and carry more risk of corrosion by letting water into the joint.

Swaged connections are made by inserting the end of the rod or cable into the tubular end of the fork or eye and then forcibly compressing the latter to a smaller diameter between rollers, thus forming a waterproof joint that is stronger than the tendon itself. The operation can be done on site with portable equipment and is possible with tendon diameters of up to about 26 millimetres. The method is economical and popular but does not allow adjustment, and additional threaded fittings are required for shortening or lengthening.

Welded connections are only used with solid rods of large diameter. These, too, do not allow adjustment and additional threaded fittings are required to allow for shortening or lengthening.

CANOPY MAINTENANCE

CLEANING

PVC coatings tend to pick up dirt and are best avoided in urban or other dirty atmospheres. They must be regularly cleaned to avoid loss of translucency and unattractive appearance (though thin surface finishes may alleviate the problem). But the more they are cleaned the more they will be embrittled by contact with soaps, solvents and oils. There is no real solution to this problem except to ensure that cleaning is carried out exactly to the manufacturer's instructions using soft brushes, water and mild detergent.

PTFE coatings tend to remain clean as dust particles do not stick and are washed away by rain. PTFE-coated glass fabric also shows no tendency to discolour with age and remains white. Cleaning is therefore less important than with PVC-coated membranes. In permanent structures of both coating types access for cleaning should be considered at design stage.

REPAIR

Small tears or damage due to vandalism can usually be repaired on site. Large tears should be referred to the manufacturer/installer, who may wish to remove the canopy for repair. Reputable manufacturers/installers will supply a maintenance and cleaning manual for permanent structures.

RE-TENSIONING

The manufacturer/installer should return to the site six months after erection to test whether re-tensioning is required. It is unlikely that further re-tensioning will be needed, especially for glass fabrics.

CABLE INSPECTION

Cables in external situations are subject to corrosion and should be regularly inspected, particularly where they enter fixings such as forks or eyes, and especially if they have plastic sheaths which hide what is happening underneath.

COST

At 1995 prices the erected cost of a tensioned fabric canopy including cables and supporting steelwork was approximately £160 to £240 per square metre (PVC-coated polyester) and £240 to £400 (PTFE-coated glass). Equivalent costs for the fabric alone would be approximately £60 to £130 (PVC-coated polyester) and £160 to £220 (PTFE-coated glass). The longer life and lower cleaning costs of PTFE-coated glass must, of course, be taken into account when comparing these figures. Large simple structures will be at the lower ends of these ranges, small complex structures at the upper ends (or even higher).

CONCLUSION

Tensioned fabric structures offer the possibility of delight both to professional designers and to the millions of ordinary people who associate modern architecture only with brutal forms and rain streaked concrete surfaces. Soft canopies can be clean, light and delicate; their forms can be evocative of snow-capped mountains or undulating landscapes; and the combination of taut rigging and billowing canvas may bring to mind pleasant images of yachts and sailing ships.

The nautical association promises a kind of design that may even bridge that gap between theorists and the general public that has so bedevilled modern design. When in 1851 the American sculptor Horatio Greenough wrote: 'By beauty

I mean the promise of function'[1] – words that would ultimately metamorphose into the modernist manifesto 'form follows function' – he was inspired by the clipper ship. And when in 1964 the novelist Norman Mailer attacked the shortcomings of modern architecture from a lay point of view, his wish was that buildings might 'begin to look a little less like armoured tanks and more like clipper ships'.[2]

'An architecture evocative of clipper ships' is a line of development worth pursuing. Stressed membrane canopies must not be thoughtlessly thrust into service wherever an 'imaginative' touch is required, but appropriately used they could lighten and enliven our landscapes and townscapes.

The problem of their proper use is not primarily technical but aesthetic. If the Greeks and the Romans had made the tent (which is after all one of the oldest and most universal forms of shelter) part of the classical canon of forms our traditional cities would no doubt be made graceful by many billowing roofs and covered ways . . . but they did not, and while we have solved the technical problems we are frankly unsure about the architectural handling of curvilinear forms relying on tensile strength and lightness rather than mass and gravity.

If this book encourages students and designers to search for the best examples worldwide, learn from them, and apply what they have learned in a principled manner, we may be a little closer to the evolution of such a language.

1. *See* James Marston Fitch, *American Building: The Historic Forces that Shaped It*, Schocken Books (New York), 1973.
2. *See* Norman Mailer, *Cannibals and Christians*, Andre Deutsch (London), 1967.

1. Prophet's Holy
Mosque, column
capital

BODO RASCH

SHADE STRUCTURES, THE PROPHET'S HOLY MOSQUE

Madinah, Saudi Arabia

Two open courtyards, each 55 x 37 metres in size, were added to the Holy Mosque. Both required some form of environmental control that would provide cooling and shelter from the sun during hot daytime periods, could be adapted to suit less hot periods, and would be visually appropriate in that setting.

Bodo Rasch's response was a group of six fabric umbrellas for each courtyard. Activated by automatic computer control, the umbrellas are hydraulically opened and closed to suit varying climatic conditions and their appearance harmonises completely with the architecture of the mosque.

When shade is required the umbrellas open in unison, the membranes gradually extending outward until the entire courtyard is covered by six translucent membranes. The action is slow, majestic and reminiscent of the opening of a flower. The space below the canopies remains entirely clear except for six slender columns.

Membrane form and material

Each umbrella opens to a maximum extent of 17.7 x 16.7 metres, with a diagonal span of 24 metres, and consists of woven PTFE (trade name Tenara) manufactured by Goretex in the USA.

The nominal plan area of each umbrella, measured across the outer tips when fully extended, is 296 square metres and the nominal spaces between the umbrellas 0.3 metres. Actual plan area of each fully extended umbrella, taking into account the scalloped edges, is 279 square metres and developed fabric area is 293 square metres.

Each umbrella is made up of forty individual panels of fabric.

Supporting structure

Columns are fabricated from steel with marble cladding and polished brass and artificial stone inserts at the capitals. Each column incorporates four cool-air outlets fed from the building's air-conditioning system and four lamps for night-time illumination. The latter are incorporated at the column capitals.

The spokes which raise and extend the membranes are fabricated from ultra-high strength steel. The operation is much like that of an umbrella but in reverse: the upper section of the mast is pulled downward (rather than pushed up) by an hydraulically operated system which then pushes the arm-tips outwards, stressing the membrane.

SUMMARY DATA

Client:
CTHM King Fahd Bin Abdul Aziz for the Kingdom of Saudi Arabia.

Location:
Al Madinah (Medina), Saudi Arabia.

Timetable:
Preliminary design, October 1990; construction of first prototype, November 1991; commission of twelve umbrellas, March 1992; installation completed, November 1992.

Concept and design development:
Rasch and Associates, Sonderkonstruktionen und Leichtbau GmbH, Leinfelden-Oberaichen.
Partner in charge: Dr Ing Bodo Rasch.

Project architect:
Jürgen Bradatsch.

Chief architect:
Dr Kamal Ismail, Cairo.

Fabric engineering consultants:
Buro Happold, Bath. Partner in charge, Eddie Pugh. Project engineer, Colin Gill.

Main contractor:
Saudi Binladin Group, Jeddah.

Specialist subcontractor: *SL Sonderkonstruktionen und Leichtbau GmbH, Leinfelden-Oberaichen.*

Life expectancy:
Membrane, twenty five years; supporting structure, fifty years.

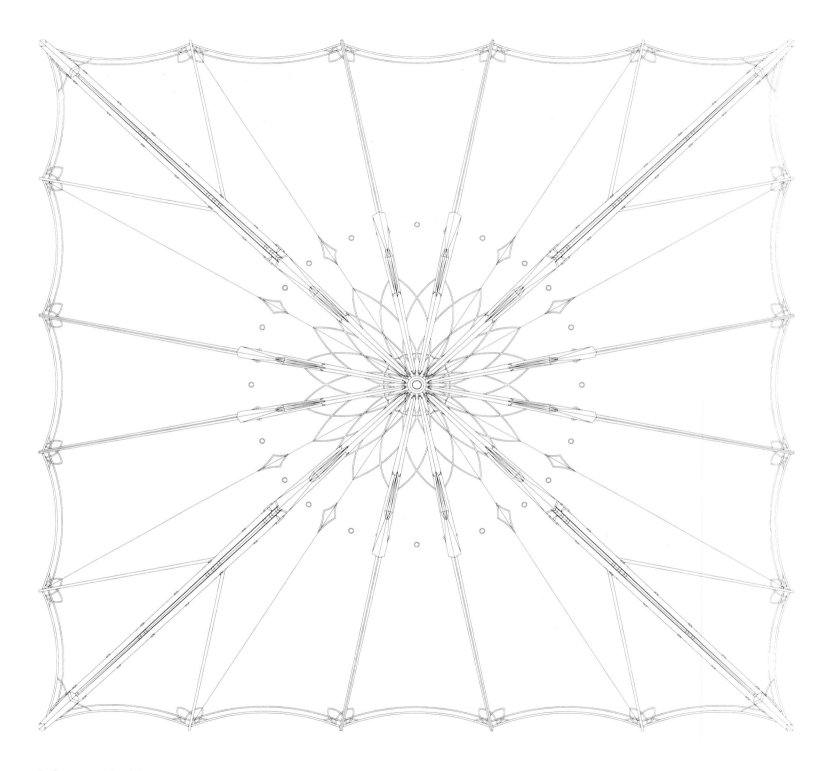

2. Canopy underside

42

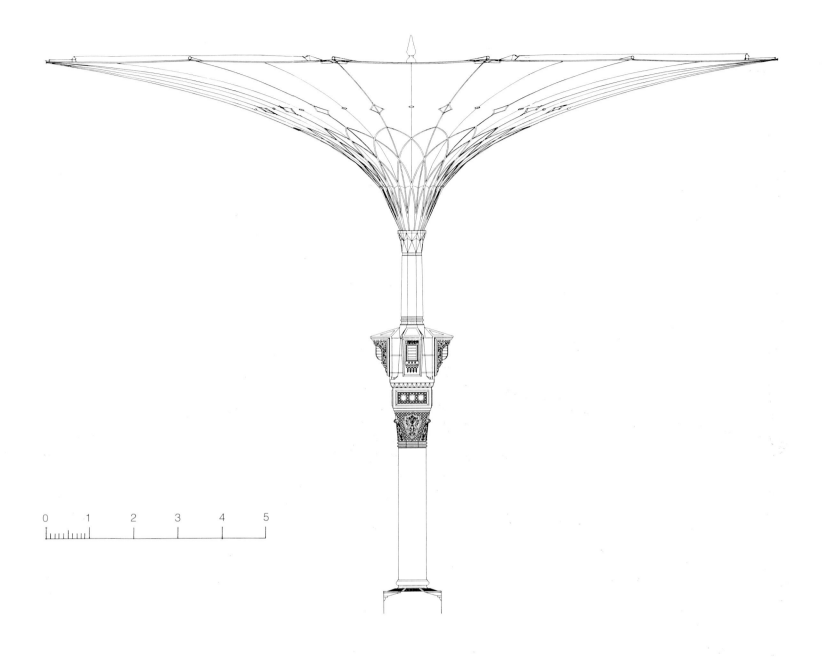

3. Elevation showing column capital and extended canopy

0 1 2 3 4 5

4. Courtyard in use

5. Courtyard with umbrellas closed; 6. Umbrellas opening; 7. Courtyard view; 8. Fully extended canopy

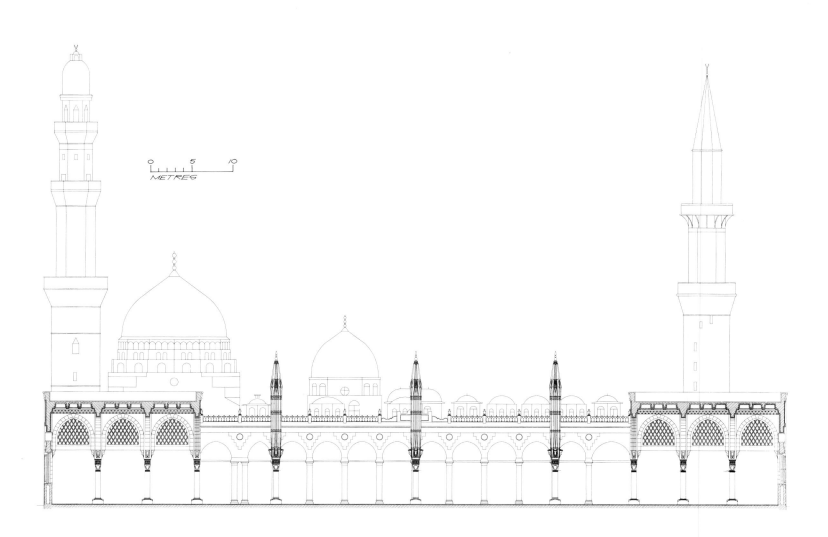

METRES

9. Cross section through courtyard; umbrellas closed

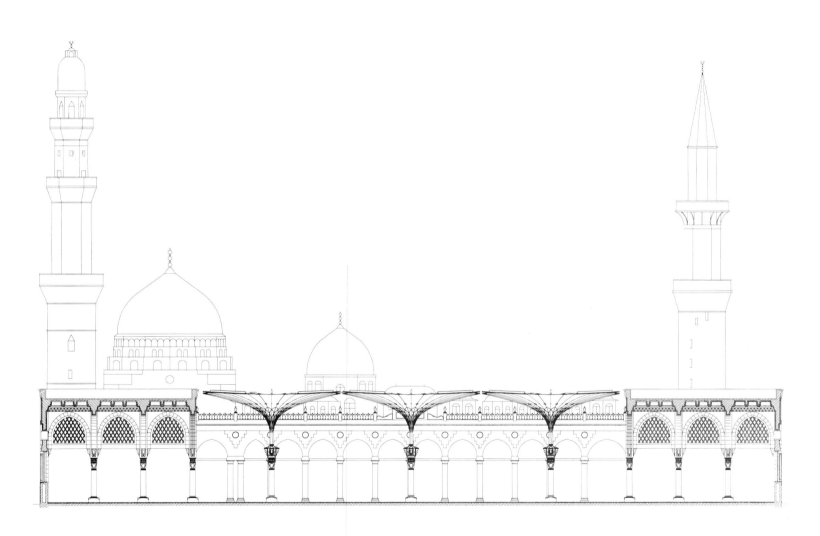

10. Cross section showing opened umbrellas

SIR MICHAEL HOPKINS AND PARTNERS

BUCKINGHAM PALACE TICKET OFFICE

London

When it was decided to open Buckingham Palace to visitors each year during August and September (while the royal family are away) the need arose for a temporary, easily erected and dismantled ticket office which could be put in storage when not in use. The design solution was a prefabricated timber cabin which is trucked to the site in two parts and then bolted together; a set of retractable jacks providing the necessary levelling. The cabin is surrounded by a sectional timber deck supported on adjustable feet, and the roof is a tented canopy. The fabric canopy is practical, being easily taken down and rolled up for storage, and also eminently eye-catching and graceful. Only the canopy is detailed here.

Membrane form and material

The canopy is formed into ridged arches in terms of the classification on page 23. The membrane takes this shape from being clamped into six curved 'coat-hangers' which are suspended from a longitudinal cable running the length of the canopy.

The membrane material is 'Velicren' fabric woven from Modacrylic yarn. Desiring a nautical appearance, the architects first proposed canvas but were advised that this would rot during the ten-month storage periods between seasons. The next option to be investigated was canvas-coloured PVC-coated polyester but the appearance was not satisfactory. Velicren, a material used mostly for awnings and yacht sails, proved to have the desired performance characteristics and appearance. The fabric has a tensile strength of 2.4 tonnes per metre in the warp direction and 1.4 tonnes per metre in the weft. Jointing is by radio-frequency welding.

Plan area is 138 square metres and the developed membrane area is approximately 159 square metres. The roof is made up of 126 individual panels of fabric. Pre-stress loads are 0.05 to 0.09 tonnes per metre (warp) and 0.04 tonnes per metre (weft).

Supporting structure

Masts and booms are made of laminated timber with oval cross sections like those of yacht spars to reinforce the nautical image. At the spar ends, stainless steel plates are spliced into the timber to take cable attachments and other fixings. Cables are stainless steel. Life expectancy for the membrane is five years; for the masts, booms and cables approximately thirty years.

Opposite: 1. Buckingham Palace ticket office, London

SUMMARY DATA

Client:
Royal Collection Enterprises, London.

Location:
Green Park, London, facing Buckingham Palace.

Timetable:
Design commenced March 1994; construction completed August 1994.

Architects:
Sir Michael Hopkins and Partners. Partner in charge: William Taylor.

Structural and fabric engineering consultants:
Ove Arup and Partners.

Partner in charge: John Thornton.
Analysis and cutting patterns:
Tensys and David Wakefield.

Construction co-ordinator:
Laing Management.

Main Contractor:
Holloway White Allom.

Fabric subcontractor:
Landrell Fabric Engineering Limited.

Cost of canopy at 1994 prices:
overall £28 000; cost/m² £167.

2. Canopy underside

3. Mast junction

4. Scalloped canopy edge

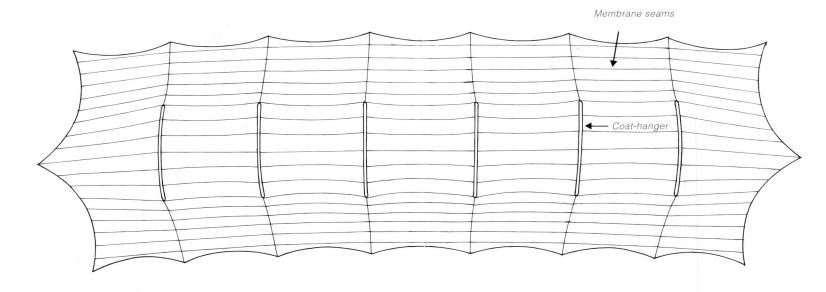

Membrane seams

Coat-hanger

5. Plan above canopy

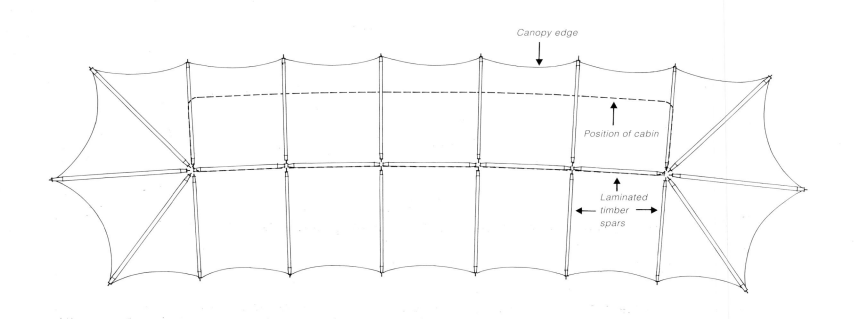

Canopy edge

Position of cabin

Laminated timber spars

6. Plan at spar level

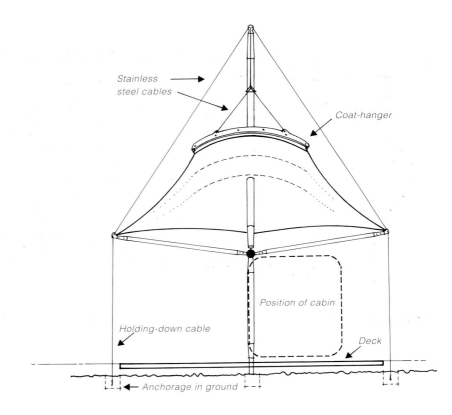

Stainless
steel cables

Coat-hanger

Position of cabin

Holding-down cable

Deck

Anchorage in ground

7. Cross section

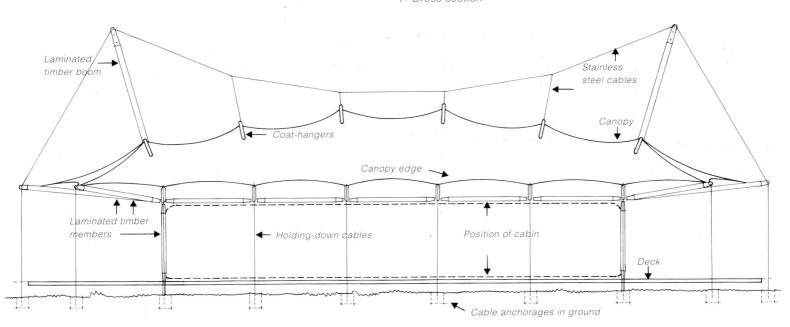

Laminated
timber boom

Stainless
steel cables

Coat-hangers

Canopy

Canopy edge

Laminated timber
members

Holding-down cables

Position of cabin

Deck

Cable anchorages in ground

8. Longitudinal elevation

1. Carlos Moseley Pavilion,
New York

FTL ASSOCIATES

CARLOS MOSELEY PAVILION

New York

The requirement was for a portable, completely self-contained stage and performance shell that could be erected at a different New York park each night during the summer, providing a top quality visual and acoustic performance venue. The brief indicated that the components should be transportable via ordinary city streets with no need for special highway permits; be erectable in six hours on uneven sites and be dismantled even more quickly; and leave natural grass sites completely undamaged.

The design response is a kit of parts consisting of five conventionally-sized trailers all of which, together with the equipment they carry, become part of the venue structure. All the trailers conform fully with federal highway weight and dimensional limitations which specify a 4 metre maximum height and 13.7 metre maximum depth for each trailer bed plus cargo.

This portable stage is capable of erection on any site that is firm, reasonably level, and accessible to the trucks.

Kit of parts

a. A platform trailer carrying the folded stage in two halves and, stored between them in folded condition, the rear canopy truss.
b. A trailer carrying the left front canopy truss.
c. A trailer carrying the right front canopy truss.
d. A trailer carrying the sound towers plus a fork-lift truck for conveying the towers to their positions on the site.
e. A trailer carrying the fabric canopy plus lighting equipment.
f. A truck carrying the electrical distribution.
g. A truck carrying carrying all props.

Erection sequence

The sequence can be broken into the following stages:
1 The platform trailer A is the first to arrive on site.

2a Trailer A is parked behind the intended platform position (locating itself very accurately by laser transit) and levels itself by means of hydraulically-operated feet. *2b* Three aluminium beams are extended from each side of the trailer by hydraulic pistons and are levelled. *2c* The four corner trailers back up to the aluminium frame (again located by laser transit) and are attached to the frame.

3a The two front trusses are lifted a few degrees to allow the plywood stage panels to unfold. *3b* The plywood stage folds out along the aluminium rails until it forms a completely flat surface 12 x 24 metres in size. The fully extended platform rests on the aluminium rails, the trailer bed of truck A at its rear centre, and the trailer beds at its four corners. The trailers are weighted with concrete ballast to counteract the forces generated by tensioned membrane and superstructure, and stabilised by hydraulically operated adjustable foot pads.

4a The two front trusses are unfolded to their full 26 metre lengths and attached to the rear truss. *4b* The rear truss is hydraulically unfolded to its full height, raising the two front trusses to an apex 21 metres high. When the final pyramidal geometry is achieved the joint at the apex is secured by a sliding steel pin. *4c* The front trusses carry the main theatrical lights which are permanently wired in.

5 The fabric membrane is unrolled on the stage, connected to the tractors at the four stage corners, winched up into position, and tensioned to form the correct saddle-shaped surface. A 4.8 metre diameter circular fabric screen is suspended above the membrane for video projection of images or surtitles. An aluminium truss is assembled on stage and hoisted up to carry overhead lighting to supplement the light fittings mounted in the front trusses.

6 A forklift (with special balloon tyres to avoid damaging the turf) carries the twenty-four speaker towers to their locations. Each speaker is then raised on extendable legs to a height of 4.8 metres for effective sound projection.

7 Acoustic reflector panels made of plywood-faced aluminium are installed on stage, lighting and sound are checked, and stage props are positioned.

After an erection process that has taken four to six hours the stage is completely ready to receive the musicians.

Performance

Visually, the saddle-shaped canopy provides a strong focus – particularly when illuminated from below at night by the computerised lighting system.

Acoustically, twenty-four speaker units electronically mimic the characteristics of an enclosed auditorium. Sound is received by stage microphones, transmitted to a mixing console 60 metres from the stage, and then broadcast to the self-contained, battery-operated speakers standing in concentric rings round the audience. Sound intensity from the front speakers is greater than from those at the rear (so that the sound is experienced as emanating from the stage) and a slight delay is induced in the sound emitted from the rear speakers to model the effect of reflected sound from the rear walls of a concert hall.

There is also some reflection of natural sound towards the audience by the aluminium, plywood-faced reflectors on the stage.

Membrane form and material

The canopy is a doubly-curved surface made of 1.9 millimetre thick polyester fabric (Ferrari type series 1002S) with a strip tensile strength of 7.7 tonnes per metre in the warp direction and 7.63 tonnes per metre in the weft direction. The fabric is coated on both sides with a PVC finish that is 350 microns thick on the top yarns. Fabric joints are radio-frequency welded.

The canopy perimeter is formed by a 19 millimetre diameter Kevlar rope wrapped in fabric sleeves. The flexibility of this synthetic fibre allows the rope to be left in place as the canopy is rolled up, thus saving 45 to 60 minutes on the erection time that would be needed if a steel cable were used (as the latter would have to be removed each time the canopy was rolled up). However Kevlar is less durable than steel and the rope must therefore be replaced every two years.

The canopy is made up of six individual fields totalling fifty-two cloth panels each of which has a nominal width of 1.68 metres. Pre-stress load varies between 0.029 and 0.146 tonnes per metre in both warp and weft directions. Canopy plan area is 277.12 square metres and developed fabric area is 340.76 square metres.

Supporting structure

The trusses are of painted steel.

SUMMARY DATA

Clients:
The Metropolitan Opera; the New York Philharmonic; the City of New York's Departments of Cultural Affairs, Parks and Recreation.
Location:
Sixteen locations in New York City including the Great Lawn at Central Park, Bronx Botanical Gardens, Flushing Meadows Park and Snug Harbour.
Timetable:
Design was started in 1988 and completed in 1991; construction was completed in May 1991.
Concept and design development:
Peter Wexler of Peter Wexler Inc (theatre designers) and Nicholas Goldsmith of FTL Associates (a firm of architects specialising in lightweight structures).
Architects:
FTL Associates.

Lighting design:
Peter Wexler Inc.
Acoustic design:
Jaffe Acoustics.
Steel design:
MG McLaren.
Fabric design:
Buro Happold, New York.
Main Contractor:
Quickway Metal Fabricator.
Specialist subcontractor:
Fabric Structures Inc.
Cost of entire structure at 1991 prices:
Cost overall $3.4 million; cost/m² $12,269.
Life expectancy:
Membrane seven to ten years with regular maintenance; steel trusses twenty years.

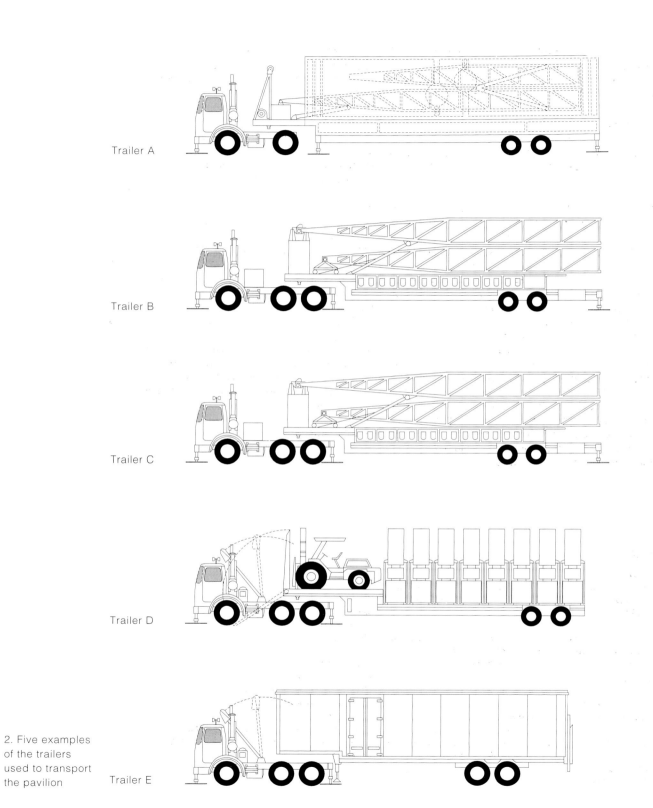

Trailer A

Trailer B

Trailer C

Trailer D

2. Five examples
of the trailers
used to transport
the pavilion

Trailer E

3. Pavilion erection sequence

Trailer A arrives
on site

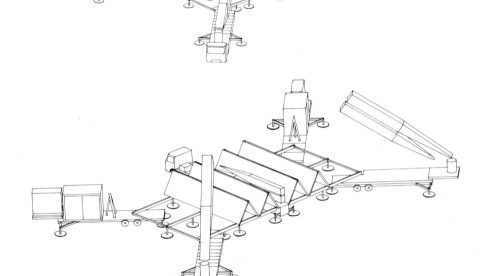

The four corner
trailers are in
position

The platform
begins to extend
and the two front
trusses are lifted
a few degrees

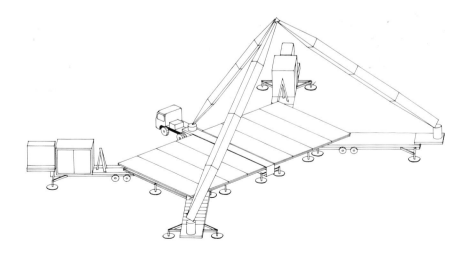

The platform is
fully unfolded and
the three trusses
fully extended

4. Completed pavilion

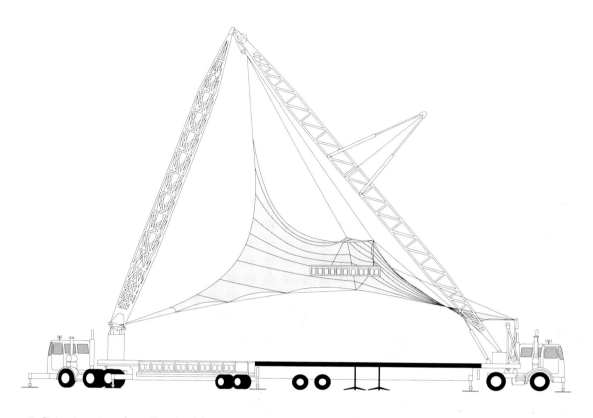

5. Side elevation of pavilion *in situ*

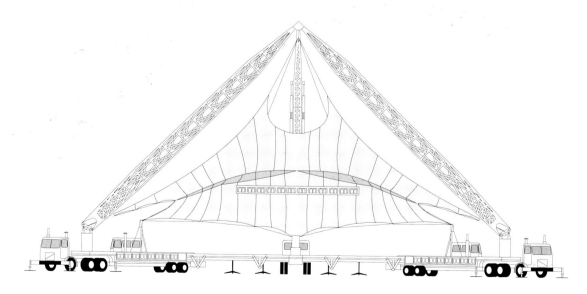

6. Front elevation of pavilion *in situ*

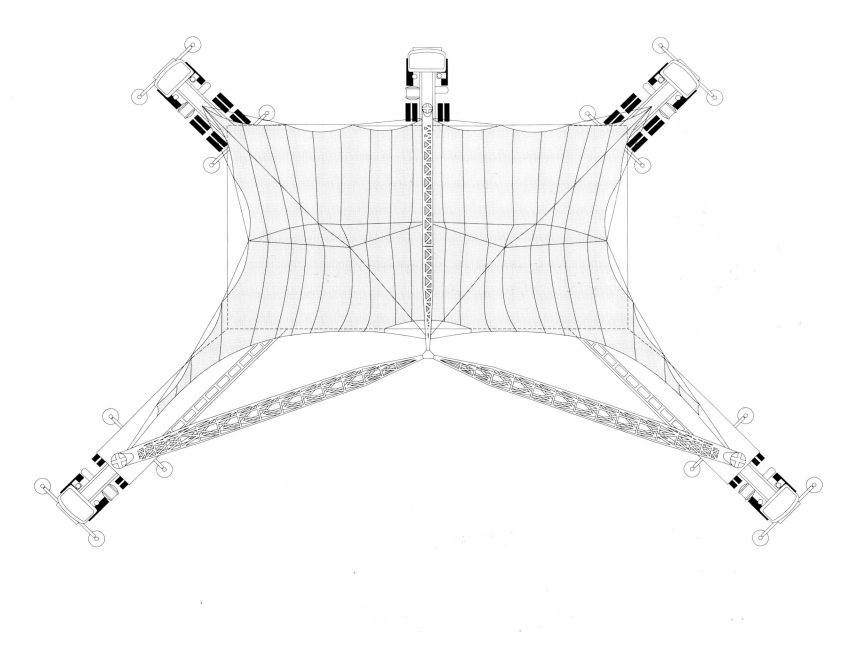

7. Overhead view of completed stadium

APPENDIX A: SPECIALIST FIRMS

The design, manufacture and installation of tensioned canopies are highly special-ised industries and it is essential to use experienced firms. The following lists are not exhaustive and are meant only as a first guide. Mostly they cover only the United Kingdom – which is not as parochial as it may seem because in the design field several British firms are acknowledged leaders, in constant demand from clients worldwide. Each list is in alphabetical order.

General design consultants:
1 Anthony Hunt Associates, Gloucester House, 60 Dyer Street, Cirencester GL7 2PF. Tel 01285 655 858.
2 Atelier One, 4 Goodge Place, London WIP IFL. Tel 0171 323 3350.
3 Buro Happold, Camden Mill, Lower Bristol Road, Bath BA2 3DQ. Tel 01225 337 510.
4 Ove Arup and Partners, 13 Fitzroy Street, London WIP 6BQ. Tel 0171 636 1531.
5 W S Atkins, Oasis Business Park, Eynsham, Oxford OX8 ITP. Tel 01865 882 828.

Form-finding and patterning:
1 Architen, Rickford, Bristol BS18 7AH. Tel 01761 462 464.
2 Tensys Limited, 7a Northumberland Buildings, Queen Square, Bath BA1 2JB. Tel 01225 445 600.

Canopy manufacturers (UK):
1 Architen, Rickford, Bristol BS18 7AH. Tel 01761 462 464.
2 Clyde Canvas, Wharton Road, Winsford, Cheshire CW7 3BY. Tel 01606 594 224.
3 Landrell Fabric Engineering Ltd, Station Road, Chepstow, Gwent NP6 5PF. Tel 01291 627 782.
4 Pagoda Space Covers, Phoenix Works, Thrupp, Stroud, Gloucester GL5 2BU. Tel 01453 886 381.

Canopy manufacturers (non-UK):
1 Birdair, 65 Lawrence Bell Drive, Amherst, New York 14221, USA. Tel 716 633 9500.
2 Canobbio, Via Spartaco 23, 20135 Milano, Italy. Tel. 551 88168.
3 Karl Nolte, PO Box 208, Eggen Kamp, D4402 Greven, Germany. Tel 2571 161.
4 Koitwerks, PO Box 27, D8219 Rimsting, Germany. Tel 8051 690 940.

Rod, cable and terminations manufacturers (UK):
1 Bridon International Limited, Carr Hill, Doncaster DN4 8DG. Tel 01302 344 010.
2 Fox's Rigging, The Strand, Wherstead, Ipswich IP2 8SA.Tel 01473 689 111
3 McCalls Special Products, P O Box 71, Hawke Street, Sheffield, S9 2LN. MSP incorporates Guy Linking. Tel 0114 242 6704.

APPENDIX B: ILLUSTRATION CREDITS

Illustrations not credited here were sketched by the author

No.	Architect	Engineer	Source
Cover	Arup Associates	Arup Associates	Arup Associates
2	–	–	Acer Consultants Limited
6	Sir Michael Hopkins & Partners	Anthony Hunt Associates;	Ove Arup & Partners
7	Frei Otto	–	Sonderkonstruktionen und Leichtbau
8	Skidmore, Owings & Merrill	URS Corporation; Geiger-Berger Associates	Skidmore, Owings & Merrill
9	Sir Michael Hopkins & Partners	Ove Arup & Partners	Ove Arup & Partners
10	Philip Cox & Partners	Ove Arup & Partners	Ove Arup & Partners
11	Renzo Piano	Ove Arup & Partners	Ove Arup & Partners
12	Arup Associates	Arup Associates	Arup Associates
13	Renzo Piano .	Ove Arup & Partners	Ove Arup & Partners
14	William Alsop	Ove Arup & Partners	Ove Arup & Partners
16	Frei Otto	Buro Happold	Buro Happold
21	Scott Tallon and Walker	Ove Arup & Partners	Ove Arup & Partners
22	Skidmore, Owings & Merrill	URS Corporation; Geiger-Berger Associates	Skidmore, Owings & Merrill
31	Arup Associates	Arup Associates	H Morrison (photographer) and Arup Associates
32	FTL/ Happold	Buro Happold	Buro Happold
37	Sir Michael Hopkins & Partners	Ove Arup & Partners	Landrell Fabric Engineering Limited; Tensys Limited
40	Renzo Piano	Ove Arup & Partners	Canobbio
42	–	–	McCalls Special Products

Case Example 1:

	Bodo Rasch	Buro Happold	Photographs and drawings: Sonderkonstruktionen und Leichtbau

Case Example 2:

	Sir Michael Hopkins	Ove Arup & Partners	Photographs: Timothy and Lorna Soar

Case Example 3:

	FTL Associates	Buro Happold	Photographs and drawings: Buro Happold

FURTHER READING

1 Bill Addis, *The Art of the Structural Engineer*, Artemis, London, 1994. A philosophical introduction plus nearly fifty short case examples illustrating a variety of structural types, including a few on tension structures. Clear and readable.

2 Philip Drew, *Frei Otto: Form and Structure*, Crosby Lockwood Staples, London, 1976. Now out of print but still one of the best-illustrated and most informative books on lightweight structures for architects.

3 John Thornton, *Tension Structures*, Royal Institute of British Architects, London, 1993. A formal teaching document for architects and students, written by a leading practitioner in the field and giving a great depth of technical and mathematical detail.